FRONTLINE
COVERAGE OF CURRENT EVENTS™

AMERICAN TROOPS IN
AFGHANISTAN

BUILDING
A NEW NATION

Philip Wolny

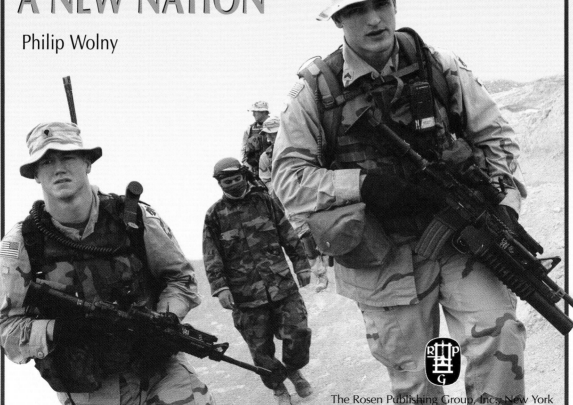

The Rosen Publishing Group, Inc., New York

Published in 2005 by The Rosen Publishing Group, Inc.
29 East 21st Street, New York, NY 10010

First Edition

Library of Congress Cataloging-in-Publication Data

Wolny, Philip.
American troops in Afghanistan: building a new nation/by Philip Wolny.—
1st ed.
    p. cm.—(Frontline coverage of current events)
Includes bibliographical references and index.
ISBN 1-4042-0343-5 (library binding)
1. Afghanistan—History—2001– —Juvenile literature. 2. War on Terrorism, 2001– —Juvenile literature. 3. United States—Armed Forces—Afghanistan—Juvenile literature. 4. Taliban—Juvenile literature.
I. Title. II. Series.
DS371.4.W67 2004
958.104'7—dc22

        2004010574

Manufactured in the United States of America

Cover images: Foreground: Members of the U.S. Army, 45th Infantry Division, on patrol in Kabul. Background: Aerial view of rugged terrain in the Bamian province, Afghanistan.

Contents

Introduction

From War to Nation-Building

A small band of soldiers hikes across a landscape of rocky hills. They follow the military Humvees that roll before them. Every now and again, an Apache helicopter buzzes overhead. Suddenly, an explosion rips across the valley. The men tense up and take cover behind the Humvees and against the stone walls. Ten minutes pass and the leader of their convoy waves them ahead. The coast is clear. The Humvees had let loose a small avalanche of rocks over a hillside. They had rolled down and set off an old land mine. A minesweeper is sent up ahead. This time, it is an old mine. But it could as easily have been an enemy fighter shooting a rocket-propelled grenade from a nearby ridge, or a suicide bomber disguised as a farmer guiding a horse-drawn cart from village to village. Nothing is ever 100 percent certain in the war zone that is Afghanistan.

Close to 3,000 people died in the September 11, 2001, attack on the World Trade Center. It was the deadliest terrorist attack on U.S. soil and the first highly lethal strike by a foreign force on the U.S. mainland since 1814. This photograph shows firefighters working in the rubble of the towers on the day of the attack.

Afghanistan is one of the many battlefronts in the worldwide war on terror that the United States declared after the September 11, 2001, terrorist attacks in New York City and Washington, D.C. The United States invaded the country in October 2001 to get at terrorists training within its borders. It quickly won the war in Afghanistan.

But since then, the uneasy peace has been unraveling. Back then, the Taliban, the group that controlled most of the country, was on the run.

Over the last two years, it has bounced back. Now many Afghans wonder whether U.S.-led coalition forces will be able to thwart its return. Taliban supporters and suspected Al Qaeda terrorists have ambushed coalition troops, international aid workers, and ordinary Afghans.

The American presence of 7,000 troops in Afghanistan is tiny compared to the occupying force in Iraq. Eighteen American soldiers lost their lives during the war in 2001. As of November 2004,

Afghanistan's future stability relies heavily on Iran and Pakistan, its two most powerful neighbors. Despite the U.S. invasion, Iran still has considerable influence in western Afghanistan, particularly in the provinces of Herat and Nimruz. Pakistan is currently engaged in joint operations with the United States in the search for Al Qaeda and Taliban leaders along the long border it shares with Afghanistan.

146 American soldiers had died in Operation Enduring Freedom.

Though international aid continues to flow in, Afghanistan seems years from being rebuilt. It is here where the battle for the hearts and minds of a war-ravaged people will count.

From helping rebuild a ruined country to rooting out guerillas, the U.S. presence in Afghanistan is crucial. What is at stake is whether Afghanistan rebuilds as a democracy, or whether it again becomes fertile ground for terrorism.

chapter 1
Winning the War, Winning the Peace

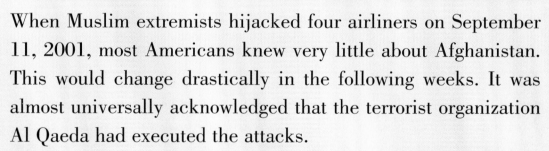

Osama bin Laden ran and financed numerous terrorist camps in Afghanistan between 1997 and 2001, when the U.S. invasion sent Al Qaeda and the Taliban on the run. Although most military and intelligence experts believe that bin Laden is now in Pakistan, they do not rule out the possibility that he may still be in Afghanistan.

When Muslim extremists hijacked four airliners on September 11, 2001, most Americans knew very little about Afghanistan. This would change drastically in the following weeks. It was almost universally acknowledged that the terrorist organization Al Qaeda had executed the attacks.

For years, Al Qaeda, under its leader, the Saudi-born billionaire Osama bin Laden, had been based in Afghanistan. It had been guests of the Taliban, Afghanistan's strict fundamentalist Muslim rulers. It was there that Al Qaeda ran camps training soldiers in a continuing terrorist war against the United States and its allies.

After September 11, the United States demanded that the Taliban turn over bin Laden and other Al Qaeda terrorists. When talks broke down, President George W. Bush decided to invade Afghanistan. He hoped to overthrow the Taliban, shut down Al Qaeda's training camps, and crush the organization.

The U.S. invasion differed from many previous American wars. The strategy involved using very few ground troops. The U.S. Air Force bombed Afghanistan first. Then, Special Forces troops and agents of the Central Intelligence Agency (CIA) were sent in to help equip and lead Afghanistan's Northern Alliance against the Taliban. The Northern Alliance was a collection of ethnic groups that had been fighting the Taliban since it took power in 1996. The Taliban itself had risen from the chaos of a civil war that raged between tribal warlords after the Soviet Union ended its occupation in 1989.

Until October 2001, the Northern Alliance controlled only 5 percent of the country. With U.S. military support, it would turn the tide. While CIA operatives handled much of the deal-making and behind-the-scenes arrangements, Special Forces often accompanied the Northern Alliance into battle.

The war was fought and won quickly. Once the outcome seemed inevitable, many Taliban fighters switched sides and joined the Northern Alliance. Thousands of Afghans, including civilians, died, and eighteen Americans lost their lives in combat. The Northern Alliance took the capital, Kabul, on November 13, 2001. The last Taliban holdout, Kandahar, a southern city, fell on December 7, to U.S. Marines.

U.S. military personnel were often suspicious of Afghans who claimed to have information on enemy fighters. Some of these were paid informants, or soldiers who

 # WHO ARE THE TALIBAN?

The Soviet Union invaded Afghanistan in 1979 to support a Communist government there. Afghan rebels fought the Soviets for the next decade. After the Soviet Union left Afghanistan, the power vacuum created a civil war. Throughout the early to mid-1990s, the nation suffered from warlord conflict. Crime, murder, and banditry were common. The Taliban (from the word *talib*, for students), were religious scholars who banded together to restore order. They were welcomed by many Afghans who lived in fear of warlord abuses. By 1996, they had taken over much of the country. They ran a strict Muslim regime. People were punished severely for minor crimes. Women had virtually no rights. Executions and amputations for breaking the rules were common. Television, music, and even flying kites were all banned for being "un-Islamic."

had until recently fought for the Taliban. It was hard to know whom to trust. In the end, the most important Al Qaeda and Taliban leaders, including Osama bin Laden, got away.

After the War

On May 1, 2002, Secretary of Defense Donald Rumsfeld announced that major combat in Afghanistan was over. But there were many things for U.S. troops to do. They needed to establish security in and around the capital city of Kabul. The United States would have to set up a temporary government until the Afghan people could democratically elect one. U.S. troops would make up the main part of the foreign troops in Afghanistan after the war. They would be joined by the ISAF, the International Security Assistance Force, made up of soldiers from twenty-nine nations.

A big part of defeating terrorism in Afghanistan is making sure it has no support there. The United States and its allies have to be watchful for the return of the Taliban and Al Qaeda. U.S. and international forces will not stay in the country forever. Also, warlords control large parts of the country, sometimes fighting each other. For these reasons, Afghanistan needs a strong central government.

Milestones

With the Taliban overthrown and Al Qaeda on the run, the Northern Alliance occupied the cities of Kabul and Kandahar. The question of who would run postwar Afghanistan became pressing. The United States and its allies knew they had to find a leader who could appeal to all the ethnic and political groups in the country.

An international conference was held in Bonn, Germany, to decide on an interim (temporary) government. Delegates of the Northern Alliance and Afghan exile groups attended. There were intense debates over leadership and peacekeeping duties.

On December 5, 2001, the delegates at the convention selected a Pashtun leader, Hamid Karzai, to be interim president. This was largely due to U.S. support. But he was also a respected former mujahideen (anti-Soviet guerilla) acceptable to most ethnic groups.

The Bonn Agreement also laid out the immediate future of security in Afghanistan. An international coalition would contribute between 3,000 and 5,000 troops to patrol Kabul. It would be led by the British. This would become the ISAF. It would later fall under the control of the United Nations (UN). The Americans would continue to root out the Taliban and Al Qaeda.

Afghan delegates of the international conference in Bonn, Germany, participate in a round-table discussion about the future of Afghanistan on November 11, 2001. The conference included four delegations: the Northern Alliance; the Cypress group, made up of exiles with ties to Iran; the Peshawar group, Pashtun exiles in Pakistan; and the Rome Group, loyalists of former Afghan king, Mohammad Zaher Shah. Four of the thirty-two delegates were women. Eighteen countries sent representatives to monitor the talks.

Many had gone into hiding or had fled to the border region next to Pakistan, or elsewhere.

The Rise of Hamid Karzai

Hamid Karzai, born in Kandahar, was a member of a Pashtun clan called the Populzai. During the Soviet occupation in the 1980s, he gave money to the mujahideen and fought the Soviets on the battlefield. When the Soviets left, he served as deputy foreign minister in Afghanistan before the civil war erupted. At first, he supported the Taliban because it brought stability. He soon opposed it. He felt that it was being controlled by Islamic fundamentalists and renegade members of Pakistan's Directorate for Inter-Services Intelligence (similar to the CIA).

When the Taliban offered Karzai a government post, he turned it down. In 1996, Karzai fled to Quetta, Pakistan, because he feared his days were numbered. From there, he worked to overthrow the Taliban.

When the United States began air strikes on October 7, 2001, Karzai saw his opening to return home. He sneaked across the border and started an anti-Taliban revolt outside Kandahar. Secret American airlifts of supplies and weapons kept his growing rebellion alive. Within weeks, Operational Detachment Alpha (ODA) 574, a Special Forces team of eleven men, had joined Karzai and his troops. With more air support, Karzai and ODA 574 fought back 1,000 Taliban at Tarin Kowt. Despite heavy resistance, Karzai and his team helped take Kandahar, the last city in Taliban hands.

During the conflict, Karzai was told by telephone that the Bonn conference had elected him the interim president. He was sworn into office on December 22, 2001.

The Loya Jirga

Karzai proved to be a good diplomat in the coming months. At an international donor's conference in Tokyo, Japan, in January 2002, he got pledges totalling $4 billion from many nations to help rebuild his country. In June 2002, a loya jirga was convened. The loya jirga is an Afghan tradition that brings together leaders from all ethnic groups to decide national issues. The June loya jirga reappointed Karzai as interim leader.

One of Karzai's most important accomplishments was the constitutional loya jirga. The meeting convened in December 2003 and included 502 delegates from the country's many ethnic

This photograph shows the presiding officers of the constitutional loya jirga during the third session of the meeting in Kabul on December 16, 2003. Sibghatullah Mojaddedi (*second from right*), the former president of Afghanistan, chaired the session. Three rockets landed near the site of the loya jirga's white tent that day.

groups. The debates over women's rights and how much influence Islam would play in the constitution were intense.

The constitution was approved on January 4, 2004. It called for direct presidential elections and a two-chamber national assembly, much like the U.S. Congress. A system of civil law was established. However, no law would go against Islam. Women were given equal rights as citizens. A quarter of all seats in the lower house of the parliament were guaranteed to women as well. Also, minorities were granted full rights in their respective areas, including the

freedom to use and teach their languages. This was a great victory for those who feared that the Pashtuns would dominate. The Pashtuns make up 40 percent of the population. They are Afghanistan's largest ethnic group.

Karzai's Turn

Karzai's rise to the presidency has been both praised and criticized. Some international observers see him as a U.S. puppet. This is because without the United States and the UN, his government does not have a military to resist the warlords that more or less control Afghanistan. He has little real

President Hamid Karzai *(right)* signs Afghanistan's new constitution into law during a ceremony at the Ministry of Foreign Affairs in Kabul on January 26, 2004. Beside him is former Afghan king, Mohammad Zaher Shah.

power if the warlords decide to oppose him. Others see him as a puppet of the Northern Alliance.

Generally, Karzai is widely accepted. As a Pashtun, he has a political base of roughly 40 percent of the population. As a former mujahideen, he is acceptable to most warlords. He is also a longtime ally of the Northern Alliance. One of his major selling points is that he was not involved in Afghanistan's civil war. However, he will need a great deal more than his popularity to glue the country back together.

A Road for Unity

One important milestone for Afghan reconstruction was the reopening of a highway between Kabul and Kandahar on December 16, 2003. Destroyed by twenty years of war,

The reopened Kabul-to-Kandahar highway is one of the most visible successes of the American effort to rebuild Afghanistan. The 300-mile (483-kilometer) highway is the country's main route. About one-third of the population lives within 30 miles (48 km) of the highway. This photograph shows Afghans walking along the highway on the day it was reopened.

the highway's reopening was a moment of pride for Karzai and many Afghans. The travel time between Afghanistan's two largest cities was cut from two days to about five hours. This will be invaluable for the economy. It also gives Afghans confidence in their new government. Nevertheless, Afghanistan's lack of good roads is perhaps not its biggest hurdle. Instead, it is the struggle between the way of the warlords and the new path of the Karzai government.

To make it easier for the fledgling government, U.S. troops are helping to rebuild Afghanistan and its armed forces. They also seek to win the hearts and minds of the people in order to gain their support against Al Qaeda terrorists.

chapter 2
Hearts, Minds, and Military Might

A U.S. Army Special Forces operative shows an Afghan National Army recruit how to hold a gun during target practice in Kabul on May 26, 2002. The new Afghan army is being trained by U.S., British, and French forces. Its main responsibility will be border security.

At the end of the war, Afghanistan was a country with no real government or military. U.S. forces are undertaking many crucial tasks to convert Afghanistan into a functioning democracy. However, there are many stumbling blocks to nation-building.

A queue of young Afghan men wait to register to join the military at the National Army Training Center in Kabul on February 18, 2004. In addition to training recruits, the United States provides uniforms and basic equipment to the Afghan National Army. Former Soviet–bloc countries supply the weapons.

The Afghan National Army

One of the most important goals is to create a national army. The United States began training recruits for the Afghan National Army (ANA) in early 2003. It hopes that the ANA will eventually protect Afghans from terrorist attacks and reduce the power of the warlords. There are up to 100,000 soldiers in warlord militias. The eventual goal is to disarm these men and return many of them to civilian life. Currently, only the Americans and the ISAF stand between the warlords and Karzai. It is widely believed that they would take advantage if given the chance.

The United States hopes to train up to 70,000 men before it turns over security to the central government. Although recruitment and training are behind schedule, there has been some progress. As of October 2004, the ANA numbered about 16,000 soldiers.

Challenges

The United States hoped to draw army recruits from all of Afghanistan's ethnic groups. However, some warlords have been reluctant to donate their own troops. Two of the most powerful, Abdul Rashid Dostum and Ismail Khan, flatly refused to do so. Diversity is even more difficult to achieve because of cultural and language barriers. For example, Pashtuns speak Pashto, while much of the training is given in the national language, Dari.

In addition, many recruits are illiterate. This has forced U.S. trainers to improvise. The training of combat medics, for example, often does not include textbooks. Describing a typical training session, Staff Sergeant Carl Petersen, a member of the ten-man Army Center for Health Promotion and Preventive Medicine stationed in Pol-e-Charkhi, says, "We show them, then they have to repeat the process," according to the Army News Service. The recruits later perform their exams by showing as well.

U.S. forces are trying to make training more efficient. By making some of the more experienced recruits officers and trainers themselves, they hope to speed the army's growth. Though many of the recruits have combat experience, they are poorly trained. In addition, the trainers must work hard at gaining the trust of the recruits.

Hearts and Minds

Convincing Afghans of American goodwill is a big part of what U.S. troops do every day. U.S. troops hope that if they help a village, the villagers may be less likely to help anticoalition guerillas and more willing to provide valuable information to American forces.

On one hand, there are individual efforts. Captain Scott R. Cadieux of the Vermont Guard's 124th

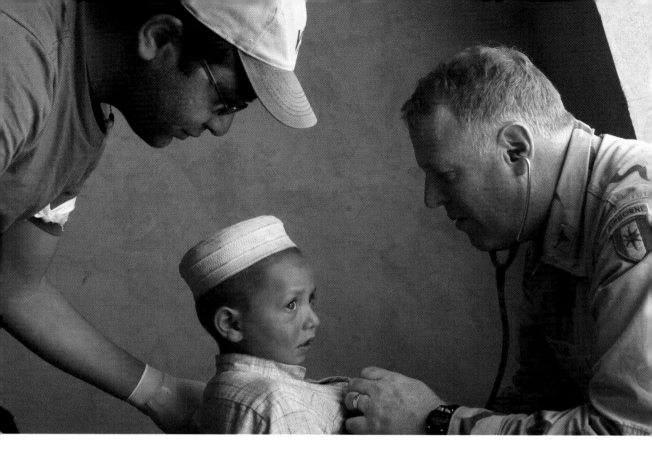

A member of the Provincial Reconstruction Team examines an Afghan boy at a temporary field hospital in Mulan (near Gardez), Afghanistan, on April 14, 2003. The hospital was set up in one night and was used for forty-eight hours. American military doctors work closely with Afghan doctors as they move around the country to provide health care.

Regional Training Institute (RTI), stationed in Kabul, started Operation Sandbox. As part of this effort, Cadieux and some of his fellow soldiers have gone to local orphanages and given food, toys, clothing, and blankets to about 3,000 children. The supplies were donated by friends and family of the 124th RTI.

Provincial Reconstruction Teams (PRTs)

On a wider scale, the military has created Provincial Reconstruction Teams (PRTs). For a while, there was criticism that the United States and ISAF had abandoned the Afghan countryside and outer provinces. The PRTs were created

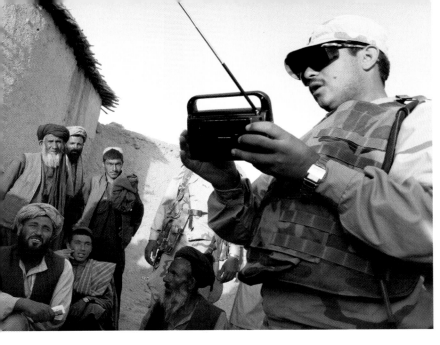

A member of the U.S. Civil Affairs Unit shows the features of a radio to a group of Afghan men in the village of Goranda, near the Pakistan border, on April 24, 2003. The U.S. Army distributes radios and other items in a continuing effort to court the goodwill of the villagers.

to help extend the power of the central government and provide much-needed security.

A PRT is made up mainly of soldiers, but it includes civilians. PRTs may include engineers, agricultural advisers, and translators, among many other experts. First launched in Kabul in late 2002, it was hoped that the PRTs would speed along reconstruction. Unlike most U.S. military units that move around Afghanistan, PRTs stay in one place for a long time.

A PRT will set up base in a local area and help rebuild a school, build a hospital, repave roads, or dig wells. They also help protect non-governmental organizations (NGOs) such as the Red Cross or the United Nations Children's Fund.

The U.S. Army runs a PRT in the area of Gardez. It includes members of the 82nd Airborne Division, Army Civil Affairs, and some members of Special Forces. They opened a storefront in the town where residents may go for assistance. This is called a Civil-Military Operations Center (CMOC). Some local Afghan leaders have praised the new PRT. Before the PRT was established, an aid organization came and distributed food to villagers. Later,

SPECIAL FORCES MISCUES

Sometimes, confusion results from the troops' changing role in Afghanistan. According to a *Washington Post* article, this confusion may have let certain "high-value targets" escape capture. The fugitive leader of the Taliban, Mullah Mohammad Omar, was reportedly sighted at a mosque in Kandahar in early 2004. A Green Beret base, Firebase Gecko, was alerted. However, official military procedure dictated that Delta Force be called on to catch him. But Delta Force was hundreds of miles away. By the time it was ready, Omar was long gone. A similar event occurred when one of Osama bin Laden's deputies, Ayman al-Zawahiri, was seen in Gardez. A Green Beret unit, only five minutes away, had to sit by and wait for SEAL Team Six to show. Meanwhile, al-Zawahiri fled.

they found that a local warlord had confiscated the food. With PRTs in place, such abuses can be prevented. Also, they help build confidence in the Karzai government.

The United States recently expanded the PRTs into southern and eastern Afghanistan. These are areas where violent pro-Taliban forces have made it dangerous for relief organizations to set up operations. In doing so, the army hopes that aid workers will return to these areas.

Downsides

In a country of 20,000,000 people, the PRTs can seem like just a drop in the bucket. They are not allowed to stop human rights abuses. They also don't have the authority to stop fighting between rival warlords.

Aid groups have also questioned the role of the PRTs. For example, in late October 2003, Paul Barker, country director for CARE International, a global anti-poverty organization, told Agency France-Presse that the PRTs are "an inadequate response to a very complex security situation." Many aid groups think that the PRTs hurt their own cause. They believe that Afghans will identify humanitarian relief with military occupation. In addition, they question putting new PRTs into relatively safe areas. They believe that the military

 **THE SCARS OF WAR**

The situation for the Afghan people is grim. According to recent reports from the World Health Organization (WHO), as many as half of all Afghan children are malnourished. Perhaps two out of three Afghans have no health care. Even in Kabul, where there has been the most progress, there's only one doctor for every 1,000 people. In Bamian Province, the ratio is one for every 100,000. Afghanistan has one of the world's highest rates of mothers dying in childbirth. Life expectancy for most people is about forty-five years.

The scars of war are both physical and mental. Afghanistan is still covered with millions of land mines left over from past conflicts. Dozens of people die monthly, while many more are seriously injured from stepping on mines.

For those who escape death and injury, there are few prospects for work. The economy is slowly getting off the ground. However, many young men have known only war. It will be a painful transition to democracy, if it happens at all.

should concentrate on security and let the NGOs worry about rebuilding the country—a task they claim they can do more cheaply and efficiently.

Security is the biggest obstacle to rebuilding. Increasingly, NGOs are the targets of deadly attacks. More than thirty aid workers have been killed in Afghanistan since the beginning of 2003 by suspected Taliban supporters. In November 2003, a French UN worker was shot in the face and killed in the southern town of Ghazni. At least four workers were killed in Taliban ambushes while building the Kabul-to-Kandahar highway. On August 2, 2004, two aid workers were shot dead on a road outside of Kabul. A major blow to aid operations in Afghanistan was the indefinite withdrawal of Medecins Sans Frontieres (Doctors Without Borders), following the death of five of its staff after an attack in the northwestern part of the country in June. Doctors With-

Lieutenant Colonel Bryan Hilferty is the senior spokesman for the U.S. military in Afghanistan. He is pictured here speaking at a news conference in Kabul on March 19, 2004, at which he confirmed the deaths of two American soldiers during a firefight in Oruzgon Province in central Afghanistan.

out Borders had maintained a presence in the country for twenty-four years, through the Soviet occupation and the civil war of the 1990s.

Caught in the Crossfire

In their efforts to provide security, American troops have made some fatal mistakes. One unintended tragedy occurred during a U.S. attack on a suspected terrorist

Lieutenant General David Barno has been commander of the U.S.-led forces in Afghanistan since October 2003. Many observers say that his diplomatic style has greatly advanced Afghanistan's march toward democracy.

Upon his selection to command the coalition forces in Afghanistan, he was named lieutenant general. Two months after assuming command in Afghanistan, Barno predicted that Osama bin Laden would be captured by the end of 2004. He has since backed off that prediction.

compound in Gardez on December 5, 2003. Lieutenant Colonel Bryan Hilferty told CNN that the target was an anti-American Afghan commander who was hiding weapons. However, six children and two adults were found crushed beneath the rubble.

Only a week before that incident, an A-10 attack aircraft killed a man in the village of Petaw. U.S. officials said at first that the man targeted was Mullah Wazir, a former Taliban leader. However, nine children were also killed during the attack.

Many Afghans are cooperating with the United States. Some simply need work, but others do so out of a sense of patriotism. Afghan soldiers assisting U.S. troops hunting terrorists are in particular danger. Interpreters, drivers, and other cooperative Afghans are regularly threatened and intimidated. Seen as traitors by anticoalition forces, they have been attacked and killed by the dozens.

chapter 3

Warlords: A Stumbling Block

Afghan villagers drive by U.S. troops on Operation Valiant Guardian (the mission to find Al Qaeda and Taliban forces), in the village of Loy Kariz on April 24, 2003. The United States is disappointed with the limited support Afghan warlords have given to such operations.

One of the biggest problems facing Afghanistan is the rule of the warlords. With only about 16,000 trained soldiers in its army, the Karzai government only has political power. True power in Afghanistan comes at the barrel of a gun. Karzai and his backers hope to change that, but that will be difficult.

This will be especially hard because the United States has worked with and supported the warlords from the beginning of the war. Army 5th Special Forces Group teams, ODA 595 and 555, two teams of twelve men each, were among the first U.S. soldiers on the ground in Afghanistan. Each team joined with a different Northern Alliance warlord: 595 with Adbul Rashid Dostum, and 555 with Mohammed Atta. Both groups joined forces in November 2001, in the siege of Mazar-e-Sharif, a Taliban-held city in northern Afghanistan.

With so few U.S. troops on the ground, it was hard to keep the warlords in check. When the Northern Alliance made it to Kabul, it had promised General Tommy Franks and other U.S. commanders that it would not enter the city. But when the Taliban ran, the Northern Alliance forces occupied it.

The Warlords in a Time of "Peace"

When relative peace was restored to Afghanistan, the United States concentrated on tracking down escaping Al Qaeda and Taliban members. Many had blended into the population. The warlord militias were the only ones who could help U.S. troops in their mission.

But there was a big problem with this alliance. The warlords threaten Afghan security almost as much as the Taliban and Al Qaeda do.

Human Rights Watch (HRW) is an organization that works to stop human rights abuses worldwide. It has released several reports that blame the warlords for much of the crime in Afghanistan today. It also blames them for returning women to the status they had under Taliban rule: second-class citizens living in fear. Moreover, many journalists and political groups have also been terrorized by warlords.

Abuses

In the years since American audiences first saw women shed their burkas in news footage from a liberated Afghanistan, many areas in Afghanistan are going backward. The new freedoms that women briefly enjoyed after the Taliban fell are lacking in many places. Many women are afraid to work, or to send their daughters to school. Roving bandits attack and rob homes, often raping women, girls, and even boys. Often, these are militia members loyal to warlords, and their crimes go unpunished.

In December 2002, HRW reported that Ismail Khan, the powerful warlord who ruled the western province of Herat, had reformed the Taliban-era Ministry of Vice and Virtue. Until September 2004, when President Karzai stripped Khan of his position as governor of Herat, this police force patrolled the streets to make sure that women did not drive cars or accompany male nonrelatives. If caught doing so, a woman was subjected to "chastity tests" to determine if she had recently had sex. In addition, schools with female students were bombed or attacked with rockets, with no investigations by the police afterward. Under Khan's leadership, women's and lawyers' groups were banned in Herat.

HRW also reports that warlords restrict free speech. Journalists who are outspoken against the warlords are often threatened, beaten, or harassed. Offices are closed down if

Warlord Ismail Khan is pictured here at a government meeting in Kabul on July 21, 2003, when he was governor of Herat. President Hamid Karzai's dismissal of Khan sparked two days of deadly riots. The riots ended only after Khan appealed to his supporters to accept the change. Khan is still considered the most powerful man in Herat.

someone writes an article critical of the warlords.

Inter-Warlord Conflict

Other events are convincing the United States that the warlords are a real threat to stability. A battle broke out on February 5, 2004, between Mayor Musadeq and a

This photograph, taken in March 2000, while Afghanistan was still under Taliban rule, shows a burka-clad Afghan woman displaying her degree. Even anti-Taliban warlords, such as Ismail Khan, continue to impose strict restrictions on women under their rule. In many areas, the central government is powerless in enforcing the constitutional right of equality for women.

local police commander, Qari Ziauddin, in Badakhstan Province, 190 miles (306 km) northeast of Kabul. Afghan troops had to step in to stop the fighting, which was reportedly over drugs. Between twelve to twenty people were killed, including civilians.

In August 2004, Ismail Khan was attacked by a neighboring rival commander, Amanullah Khan. As many as twenty fighters died during the conflict. The ANA was dispatched and eventually brokered a cease-fire. This was one of several deployments of the ANA in recent months to quell warlord fighting. However, some Afghan observers claim that the fighting in Herat was stopped more by the presence of U.S. warplanes flying overhead than any show of force by the ANA.

The United States and the Warlords

When it comes to the warlords, the United States is often caught between a rock and a hard place. Until the central government is strong enough, the United States is sometimes reluctant to enforce its laws. At the same time, it needs the support of the warlords' militias in its hunt for Al Qaeda and Taliban guerillas.

However, U.S. forces are finding it hard to trust the warlords. Some commanders suspect that warlords are feeding them false information about suspected Taliban supporters so that U.S. forces will attack their rivals. One warlord in the province of Khost, Pacha Khan Gadran used these tactics. He controlled a 3,000-man army along the border with Pakistan. U.S. forces often enlisted him and his men to hunt anticoalition forces. He refused to give up power or to accept a new governor

appointed by Karzai until he was captured in Pakistan and turned over to Afghan authorities in July 2004. He has called Karzai a puppet of the Northern Alliance and distrusts the ethnic Tajiks that dominate it.

Brad Adams, director of HRW in Asia, said in a July 2003 HRW report that "the U.S. and U.K. need to decide whether they're with President Karzai . . . or with the warlords. The longer they wait, the more difficult it will be to loosen the warlords' grip on power."

Troops on the ground have even come into conflict with some warlords. In November 2003, U.S. soldiers braved harsh terrain looking for Gulbuddin Hekmatyar and his followers. A former ally of the Northern Alliance, Hekmatyar is an Islamic fundamentalist who declared holy war against foreign troops in Afghanistan in 2002. He is believed to have befriended his former Taliban foes.

Gulbuddin Hekmatyar is a former prime minister of Afghanistan. Today, Afghanistan's government considers him a war criminal and the United States has labeled him a terrorist. He is suspected to have been behind a September 5, 2002, assassination attempt on president Hamid Karzai.

On November 6, 2003, the 10th Mountain Division's 1st Brigade began a monthlong mission called Operation Mountain Resolve in the northeastern province of Nuristan. Captain Toby Moore led his troops 22 miles (35 km) through the mountains in search of Hekmatyar. On the way, they discovered "night letters" posted on schools and mosques. They warned locals not to cooperate with U.S. troops. Moore also found villagers who said that strangers had moved into their houses and taken their food. The troops did not apprehend any enemy fighters. The locals said that any "bad men" had left days earlier.

Many operations in Afghanistan amount to such cat-and-mouse games between U.S. forces and a shadowy enemy. Because of this, the battle against Al Qaeda and the Taliban has proven to be harder than expected.

A Change in Tactics

For a long time, although the PRTs were supposed to provide security, they had no power to stop or interfere with the warlords' actions. In fact, HRW reports that in southeast Afghanistan, the "abuses by [the warlords'] gunmen were happening 'right under the moustaches' of the Americans."

U.S. soldiers prepare to search a house in Nuristan during Operation Mountain Resolve in November 2003. They were looking for Afghan warlord Gulbuddin Hekmatyar and members of his Hezbi-Islami forces.

The United States has changed some of its tactics in recent months. It has deployed about sixteen PRTs by early November 2004. The United States says these have greater power to protect regular Afghans from militia abuses. They are also being employed to help root out the drug trade in opium that is a major source of income for the warlords.

chapter 4

The Return of the Taliban and Al Qaeda

Sergeant Ryan Leonard of Bravo Company 1-87, 10th Mountain Division, mans a mounted 240B machine gun on December 3, 2003, in Patkia province, near the Pakistani border. Sergeant Leonard is part of Operation Mountain Avalanche, which searches for Al Qaeda and Taliban forces.

The conflict in Afghanistan has become a guerilla war. This means that instead of fighting enemies across a battlefield, small groups of fighters wage surprise attacks on U.S. troops. Consequently, small teams of U.S. forces patrol unfamiliar and harsh territory looking for a faceless enemy. Attackers appear and disappear quickly.

The most dangerous place for U.S. troops is in southeast Afghanistan, where Afghanistan borders Pakistan. It is also almost all Pashtun, the ethnic group that supported the Taliban the most. The border is very much open, and it is widely believed that Al Qaeda and Taliban supporters cross it to wage attacks on coalition forces.

On September 29, 2003, soldiers from the 10th Mountain Division came face to face with the enemy. Two miles (3 km) from the Pakistan border, Taliban fighters ambushed two platoons from the 1st Battalion, 87th Regiment on patrol area near their base at Shkin. A surprise mortar attack started a vicious firefight. A nineteen-year-old private was killed by sniper fire. More than twenty enemy fighters were killed.

Two months later, the 1-87 Infantry Battalion made a dangerous trek into this same area as part of Operation Avalanche. Meant to root out Al Qaeda and Taliban guerillas, it sometimes seemed like a losing battle even when U.S. troops won the skirmishes they fought.

During the mission, Staff Sergeant Mark McCallister set out to investigate an ambush that had killed two CIA agents and two Afghans five weeks earlier. He also hoped to lure enemies into a fight.

The local villagers agreed to inform the troops of the movements of the terrorists. However, the troops knew that the villagers often help whomever is in town at the moment. Many Afghans, used to years of war, have seen occupiers come and go. They fear that if the Americans leave and the Taliban return, they could be killed for helping U.S. troops.

The fight would come to other members of the 10th Mountain later that month. On December 14, 2003, 1-87's Bravo Company, the 10th Military Police Company, with medics and Afghan militia, were fired on from above. They were traveling on a road with steep walls on both sides when rocket-propelled grenades and machine-gun fire rained down on them. Soon, Apache helicopters joined the fray. Two F-16s called in to drop bombs scattered the guerillas. However, three guerillas were captured. Major Dennis Sullivan, executive officer of the 1-87, told the *Christian Science*

U.S. forces on Operation Valiant Vanguard process captured terror suspects in the village of Loy Kariz. Prisoners are interrogated for information on the whereabouts and activities of Al Qaeda and Taliban members. U.S. treatment of Afghan prisoners is being investigated in light of evidence and allegations of abuse and torture.

Monitor that the enemy "will only attack when he thinks he has a chance of success." If a big enough force comes through, the guerillas will usually pass on the chance to attack. That is why, ironically, U.S. troops send out forces just big enough to defend themselves, but small enough to lure the enemy into a fight.

The enemy is everywhere and nowhere in Afghanistan. Even when attackers are nowhere to be found, they can lay traps for U.S. forces. When troops pull into a village and the locals are strangely unfriendly (Afghans are traditionally very hospitable), they wonder whether they are surrounded by enemies who have blended in with the locals. If they receive a tip about the location of "bad men," can they trust it? When they leave, will a villager run to hiding guerillas and point them in the direction of the American convoy?

A Stealthy Enemy

Afghan guerillas have many advantages over U.S. troops. Though American troops are better trained and have superior weapons, anticoalition Afghans have a home-field advantage. They know the land, the people, and how to move around.

Enemy fighters also use disguises. Some wear traditional Afghan clothes under black tunics, which they can drop along with their weapons. Others hide weapons under civilian clothes until they are close enough to ambush coalition soldiers.

In addition, the terrorists hide weapons in different villages. Some guerrillas have taken refuge in fake walls and behind sliding doors in the homes of sympathetic villagers.

In the cities, enemy fighters can blend in just as easily. Staff Sergeant Dick of the 2nd Battalion of the 19th Special Forces, Army National Guard (for security reasons, Special Forces can reveal only their first names to journalists), is based in Kunduz. He points out the case of Daud Khan, a local warlord allied to the Special Forces. Khan's militiamen are supposed to be chasing Al Qaeda. But it's been discovered that one of his militia has been hiding Islamic extremist suspects from the Americans. Dick tells the *Christian Science Monitor*, "You don't know who's a good guy and who's a bad guy. But if he's shooting at you, he's definitely a bad guy."

Another Special Ops member in Kunduz, Chief Warrant Officer John, lives in a "safe house" within the city. He says that safe houses are often the target of mortar and rocket attacks. Fortunately, the aim of the attackers is poor. John carries a thermite grenade that he plans to detonate if enemy fighters enter the building and he is outnumbered.

Noncombat Casualties

Even when not battling guerillas, U.S. forces are vulnerable. Between bad weather, accidents, and other dangers, death can come from many corners.

One of the largest death tolls for U.S. troops in Afghanistan happened on November 23, 2003. Five soldiers died and seven more were injured when their helicopter crashed near Bagram Air Base. The cause turned out to be mechanical failure. Many of the maneuvers and missions involve flying troops and supplies into dangerous mountain passes. Pilots have to land on cliffs and ledges. Some of these maneuvers are so dangerous that the pilots have never been allowed to practice them in training. Pilots must sometimes limit their flying time above 10,000 feet (3,048 meters) because the air is so thin that it is hard to breathe for long periods. The terrain

FIREFIGHT IN THE BORDERLANDS

After taking surprise enemy fire on September 29, 2003, the men of the 10th Mountain Division, 1st Platoon found a wire half buried in the dirt off the road. Following the wire, Sergeant Allen Grenz crested a hill. In his sights were three enemy fighters. One was holding a detonator, another was turning toward Grenz with his gun, and the third was reaching for a grenade. It occurred to Grenz that the wire led straight to the men. With three well-placed shots fired off in less than two seconds, Grenz took down all three men. It was later discovered that the wire led to five antitank mines buried under the 1st Platoon's Humvees.

U.S. Army personnel inspect the wreckage of a U.S. MH-53 Pave Low helicopter near Bagram Air Base, 31 miles (50 km) north of Kabul on November 24, 2003. Many U.S. soldiers have lost their lives in Afghanistan as a result of helicopter crashes and other accidents.

also creates unpredictable winds and provides plenty of cover for enemies to fire upon the aircraft.

Other routine duties can also be fatal. Soldiers often capture or find weapons stores, or caches, that have been hidden by enemy forces. They are under orders to destroy these. Sometimes they have to transport weapons and explosives elsewhere to detonate them. On January 30, 2004, just west of the city of Ghazni, seven soldiers lost their lives after a weapons cache they were working next to exploded.

Beyond enemy attacks and accidents, Afghanistan can be an unforgiving place. In summer, temperatures in desert areas can reach up to 130° Fahrenheit (54° Celsius) Also, dust storms are common. During the winter, troops on patrol in the mountains brave snow, ice, and mud on exhausting hikes. Walking is often the only way to travel in some areas. Many roads were destroyed by wars. In addition, much of the countryside is unpaved or the roads are impassable by motorized vehicles.

Prospects for the Future

The war in Afghanistan rages on. With the expansion of the PRTs into more unfriendly territory, U.S. military planners have seen things intensify in recent months. Taliban attacks against Afghans and aid workers have stepped up, and elections had to be postponed twice. Representatives of the central government were successful in registering about 90 percent of the voting-age population, defying expectations. U.S. officials point out this statistic, saying that it shows Afghans' determination to create peace and democracy.

Before the election, there was a growing fear that the Taliban would cause widespread mayhem to disrupt the polls. This fear was heightened in August 2004, when the revived Taliban militia successfully detonated time bombs at a voter registration station in Farah City, and on September 16, 2004, when the Taliban tried to assassinate President Karzai by firing a rocket at a U.S. military helicopter transporting him from Kabul to Gardez.

Nevertheless, on October 9, 2004, millions of Afghans braved the threat of violence to vote in the nation's first presidential election. Election day was relatively peaceful, although there were a few skirmishes between Taliban rebels and U.S. troops. However, the election almost broke down into chaos when fifteen challengers to President Karzai accused the government of fraud, called for the election to be annulled, and threatened to boycott the election. They complained that ink used to mark people's thumbs to prove that they had already voted rubbed off too easily, thereby making it possible for people to vote multiple times.

As of this writing, the Karzai government and the United

Afghan men stand in line as they wait to vote at a polling station in Kandahar on October 9, 2004. In keeping with Afghanistan's conservative Islamic leaning, men and women voted in separate voting booths. International observers reported great optimism and enthusiasm among the millions who turned out to vote. Voter turnout, estimated to be at least 60 percent, was much higher than had been expected.

Nations are negotiating with the candidates to accept the results of the election—a victory for Karzai—which was approved by the election commission and international observers. The election dispute is significant because a democracy relies on a loyal opposition—one that accepts fair election results—to function. Whether the opposition, which includes warlords and warlord-backed candidates, accepts the legitimacy of the elected government will affect the future stability of Afghanistan.

Despite the Bush administration's declaration that the Afghan election was a triumph for democracy, a great many Afghans and U.S. military observers fear that the United States may have already missed its chance in Afghanistan. There are 150,000 troops occupying Iraq, while there are only about 18,000 in Afghanistan, a country with roughly the same population. It is easy to see how the international community might criticize the priorities of the United States.

There has been some movement to concentrate on Afghanistan more in the coming months. Pakistan, an ally of the United States in the war on terror, launched an offensive over the summer to root out Taliban and Al Qaeda supporters in the Pashtun lands bordering Afghanistan. During a recent state visit by Hamid Karzai, Pakistani president Pervez Musharaf vowed that he would do everything in his power to curb attacks originating in his country.

But support for bin Laden and anti-Americanism are strong in these border areas. Many critics charge that Pakistan's ISI and even some of its top military officials are playing both sides: launching major offensives against the Taliban yet aiding them in other ways. It remains to be seen how successful Pakistan will be.

Afghans fear that the United States will lose interest in rebuilding their country—especially if Osama bin Laden is captured. Recent news reports have implied that the United States and Pakistan are closing in on bin Laden. But there have been false alarms lately in which Pakistan claimed to have cornered major deputies of bin Laden and Mullah Omar, with nothing turning up in the end.

In July 2004, the U.S. military launched Operation Lightning Resolve. This operation involved thousands of U.S. troops who worked to keep Taliban rebels and other enemy fighters off-balance in the crucial run-up to the election. The North Atlantic Treaty Organization (NATO) also raised its troop strength from 6,000 to

8,500 in order to help maintain stability in the uncertain time of the presidential election.

Afghans' feelings about U.S. troops remain mixed. The campaign to win hearts and minds is advanced every time an irrigation ditch is dug, a road is repaved, or a school reconstructed. But accidental killings of Afghan civilians and recent allegations of abuse by U.S. troops threaten to cancel out the publicity of U.S. successes. Two prisoners died in December 2002 at the Bagram Collection Point, a detention center. The detention center was reportedly run at the time by the same military intelligence unit now charged with the abuse of prisoners at Abu Ghraib prison in Iraq from 2003 to 2004. More recently, three American mercenaries in Kabul were charged by Afghan authorities with running an illegal prison out of their private home where they allegedly beat and tortured as many as eight Afghans.

Wracked by war, Afghans have seen enemy forces come and go. They have seen many groups take power and then seen them overthrown. The stakes are extremely high for the United Sates in Afghanistan—whether the United States sticks it out will be seen as a test of how tough it will be in the wider war on terror. Many believe that the invasion of Iraq, in addition to taking away valuable troops from the front in Afghanistan, has greatly damaged U.S. efforts to win over badly needed allies in the Muslim world. How ordinary Afghans yearning for peace work out their differences and whatever role the United States plays in it will mark this part of the world for decades to come.

In the meantime, U.S. and Afghan forces will continue to die. Only time will tell if their sacrifices will bear fruit.

Glossary

Al Qaeda Umbrella term for a network of terrorist organizations widely believed to have waged attacks against the United States and its allies over the last decade, including the September 11, 2001, attacks on the World Trade Center and the Pentagon.

burka A garment worn by women in Afghanistan and other Muslim countries that covers the wearer from head to toe; a mesh screen lets the wearer see out of the garment. The burka is worn because many strict Muslims do not believe any part of a woman's body should be seen in public.

Dari One of Afghanistan's two main languages; a dialect of Persian.

high-value targets Military term for the most-wanted fugitives in Afghanistan and the war on terror.

jihad A holy war fought on behalf of Islam.

loya jirga A traditional meeting of many Afghan leaders or tribes to discuss important national matters.

mujahideen Literally "holy warriors," guerilla soldiers who fought the Soviet occupation of Afghanistan from 1979 to 1989.

mullah A religious scholar and spiritual leader for an area or group of people.

Northern Alliance A union of mainly non-Pashtun Afghan minorities from Afghanistan's north that fought and overthrew the Taliban.

Pashto The primary language of the Pashtuns.

Pashtuns The most numerous ethnic group in Afghanistan, making up about 40 percent of the population. Traditionally, the Pashtuns have led Afghanistan.

PRTs (Provincial Reconstruction Teams) Groups of soldiers and civilians deployed in a few areas in Afghanistan to provide reconstruction and security.

Tajiks One of Afghanistan's minority groups, concentrated in the northern part of the country. Tajiks have their own state in central Asia called Tajikistan.

Talib The Arabic word for student.

Taliban Islamic fundamentalist rulers of Afghanistan from 1996 to 2001.

Uzbeks One of Afghanistan's minority groups, concentrated in the northern part of the country. Uzbeks have their own state in central Asia called Uzbekistan.

warlords Military rulers in many parts of Afghanistan who command their own private armies, or militias.

For More Information

CARE
151 Ellis Street NW
Atlanta, GA 30303
(800) 422-7385
e-mail: info@care.org
Web site: http://www.care.org

Consulate-General of Afghanistan in
    New York
360 Lexington Avenue, 11th Floor
New York, NY 10017
(212) 972-2276 or (212) 972-2277
e-mail: afghancons@aol.com

Department of Defense
1000 Defense Pentagon
Washington, DC 20301

(703) 697-5131
e-mail: newsdesk@osd.mil

Doctors Without Borders/Medecins
    Sans Frontieres (MSF)
P.O. Box 2247
New York, NY 10116-2247
(888) 392-0392
Web site: http://www.doctorswith out-
    borders.org

Human Rights Watch
350 Fifth Avenue, 34th floor
New York, NY 10118-3299
(212) 290-4700
e-mail: hrwnyc@hrw.org
Web site: http://www.hrw.org

Revolutionary Association for the
  Women of Afghanistan (RAWA)
P.O. Box 374
Quetta, Pakistan
e-mail: rawa@rawa.org
Web site: http://www.rawa.org

United States Agency for
  International Development
Information Center
Ronald Reagan Building
Washington, DC 20523-1000
(202) 712-4810
Web site: http://www.usaid.gov

United States Army
U.S. Army Public Affairs Center
ATTN: SAPA-PA

Building 8607-6 ACR Rd.
Fort Meade, MD 20755-5659
Lieutenant Colonel Edward Loomis
e-mail: loomise@emh1.ftmeade.army.
  mil
Web site: http://www.army.mil/
  operations/oef/index.html

Web Sites

Due to the changing nature of Internet
links, the Rosen Publishing Group,
Inc., has developed an online list of
Web sites related to the subject of this
book. This site is updated regularly.
Please use this link to access the list:

http://www.rosenlinks.com/fcce/amta

For Further Reading

Banting, Eric. *Afghanistan: The Culture* (Lands, Peoples, and Cultures). New York: Crabtree Publishing, 2003.

Hamilton, John. *Operation Enduring Freedom* (War on Terrorism). Edina, MN: Abdo & Daughters, 2002.

Marsh, Carol. *Afghanistan: A Country at the Crossroads of War and Peace*. Peachtree City, GA: Gallopade Publishing Group, 2001.

Mirepoix, Camille, ed. *Afghanistan in Pictures* (Visual Geography). Minneapolis: Lerner Publications, 1997.

Parks, Peggy J. *Afghanistan* (Nations in Conflict). Chicago: Blackbirch Press, 2003.

Todd, Anne M. *Hamid Karzai* (Major World Leaders). New York:

Chelsea House Publishing, 2003.

Yancey, Diane. *Life of an American Soldier in Afghanistan* (American War Library). San Diego, CA: Lucent Books, 2003.

Bibliography

Agence France-Presse. "U.S. Commander in Afghanistan Says Warlords Will Face Shake-Up." Retrieved February 2004 (http://www.channel newsasia.com/stories/afp_world/ view/68240/ 1/.html).

Associated Press. "Helicopter Crash Kills 5 U.S. Soldiers." November 24, 2003. February 17, 2004. Retrieved February 2004 (http://www.usatoday.com/news/world/ 2003-11-23-afghan-crash_x.htm).

Buchbinder, David. "A Soldier's Life in Afghanistan." *Christian Science Monitor*. February 27, 2003.

Doucet, Lyse. "Afghanistan's Security Nightmare." BBC News, January 8, 2004.

Ehrenreich, Ben. "Afghanistan Revisited." *L.A. Weekly*, October 3–9, 2003.

Gall, Carlotta. "Afghan Council Gives Approval to Constitution." *New York Times*, January 5, 2004.

Gall, Carlotta. "Taliban Try to Frighten Afghan Voters in Rural Areas." *New York Times*, February 19, 2004.

Gall, Carlotta. "U.S. Military Unveils Changes in Strategy in Afghanistan." *New York Times*, December 21, 2003.

Girardet, Edward. "Afghanistan: Between War and Peace." *National Geographic*, November 2003.

Graham, Stephen. "Afghan President Signs New Constitution." Associated Press, January 26, 2004.

Graham, Stephen. "20 Afghans Die in Faction Fight." Associated Press, February 7, 2004. Retrieved February 2004 (http://www.ledger-enquirer.com/mld/charlotte/news/world/7798950.htm).

Graham, Stephen. "U.S. Death Toll in Afghanistan Reaches 100." Associated Press, January 12, 2004.

James, Michael S. "Could America Still Lose in Afghanistan?" ABC-News.com, December 26, 2003. Retrieved November 2004 (http://abcnews.go.com/International/story?id=79070&page=1).

Khan, Noor. "Afghan Village Stormed After Pilot Killed." Associated Press, February 23, 2004.

Kristof, Nicholas D. "Afghan Women, Still in Chains." *New York Times*, February 14, 2004.

Marotto, Major Wayne. "Army Reserve Soldiers Help Train Afghan National Army." Army News Service, January 15, 2004.

McGirk, Tim. "Battle in the Evilest Place." *Time*, November 3, 2003.

McGirk, Tim. "A Dearth of Troops." *Time*, December 1, 2003.

McLaughlin, Abraham. "U.S. Forces Tackle Riskier Tasks in Afghanistan." *Christian Science Monitor*, January 4, 2004.

Morrison, Dan. "Afghans' First Stab at Democracy." *Christian Science Monitor*, January 6, 2004.

Rashid, Ahmed. "Rebuilding Afghanistan." *The Nation*, January 26, 2004.

Rashid, Ahmed. "The Mess in Afghanistan." *The New York Review of Books*, January 14, 2004.

Shar, Amir. "Afghans Move to Stop Warlord Fighting." Associated Press, February 8, 2004.

Shar, Amir. "Taliban Claim Deadly Afghan Bombings." Associated Press, January 28, 2004.

Sater, Major Richard C. "Afghan National Army Training Combat Medics." Army News Service, January 26, 2004.

Tyson, Ann Scott. "Going in Small in Afghanistan." *Christian Science Monitor*, January 4, 2004.

Tyson, Ann Scott. "Uphill Pursuit for Afghan Warlord." *Christian Science Monitor*, December 22, 2003.

Williams, Staff Sgt. Timothy M. "Vermont National Guard Trains Afghan Army Trainers." American Forces Press Service, January 7, 2004.

Index

A
Afghanistan
  abuses in, 21, 26–27, 30, 31, 41
  constitution of, 12–13
  democracy and, 16, 22, 24, 38, 39
  military of, 13, 16, 17, 18, 25, 28
  Soviet occupation of, 8, 9, 11, 23
Al Qaeda, 5, 7, 8, 9, 10, 15, 26, 29, 30, 33, 35
al-Zawahiri, Ayman, 21
Atta, Mohammed, 25

B
Barno, Lieutenant General David, 24
bin Laden, Osama, 7, 8, 9, 21, 24, 40
Bonn Agreement, 10
Bush, George W., 8, 39

C
Cadieux, Captain Scott R., 18–19
casualties
  Afghan, 8, 22, 24, 28, 33, 36, 41
  aid workers, 23
  U.S., 5–6, 8, 33, 36, 37, 41
Central Intelligence Agency (CIA), 8, 12, 33
challenges
  Al Qaeda supporters, 5, 32, 40
  drugs, 27–28, 31
  food, 20–21
  guerilla warfare, 32, 33–34, 35, 36
  land mines, 4
  military procedure, 21
  suicide bombers, 4
  Taliban supporters, 5, 21, 23, 29, 30, 32, 40

  terrain, 36–37
  warlords, 13–14, 18, 20–21, 25–31, 35, 39
  weather, 37
Civil-Military Operations Center (CMOC), 20

D
Dostum, Adbul Rashid, 18, 25

E
ethnic groups, 13, 18, 32

F
Franks, General Tommy, 26

G
Gadran, Pacha Khan, 29

H
Hekmatyar, Gulbuddin, 29

I
interim government, 9, 10, 12
International Security Assistance Force (ISAF), 10, 17, 19

K
Kabul-to-Kandahar highway, 14–15, 23
Kandahar, 8, 10, 11, 12, 14, 21
Karzai, Hamid, 10, 11–12, 13–14, 15, 17, 25, 27, 29, 38, 39, 40
  criticism of, 13–14, 29
  government of, 15, 21, 25, 38
Khan, Amanullah, 28
Khan, Ismail, 18, 27, 28

L
loya jirga, 12

About the Author

Born in Bydgoszcz, Poland, at the height of the Cold War, Philip Wolny emigrated to the United States at the age of four, settling in Queens, New York. He now lives in Los Angeles, California, where he works as a freelance writer and editor.

Photo Credits

Cover © David Butow/Redux; cover (background) © Topham/The Image Works; pp. 4–5 © Steve McCurry/Magnum Photos; p. 6 © GeoAtlas; p. 7 © Corbis Sygma; pp. 11, 13, 14, 16, 27, 31, 37 © AFP/Getty Images; p. 15 © Terry Pedwell/CP/AP Wide World Photos; p. 17 © Ahmad Masood/Reuters/Corbis; p. 19 © France Keyser/In Visu/Corbis; pp. 20, 25, 34, 39 © Ed Kashi/IPN/Aurora Photos; pp. 23, 24 © Ed Wray/AP Wide World Photos; p. 28 © Nina Berman/Aurora Photos; p. 30 © Robert Nickelsberg/Liaison/Getty Images; p. 32 © AP Wide World Photos/U.S. Army, Ryan C. Creel; p. 36 © Jack Kingston/AP Wide World Photos.

Design: Geri Fletcher; Editor: Wayne Anderson; Photo Researcher: Fernanda Rocha